HEIRLOOM LANGUAGE

poems

HEIRLOOM LANGUAGE

poems

Barabara E. Young

MADVILLE PUBLISHING

LAKE DALLAS, TEXAS

FIRST EDITION

Requests for permission to reprint or reuse material
from this work should be sent to:

Permissions
Madville Publishing
PO Box 358
Lake Dallas, TX 75065

Cover Design: Jacqueline Davis

ISBN: 978-1-948692-54-0 (paperback) and
978-1-948692-55-7 (ebook)
Library of Congress Control Number: 2020941273

To Jim,
who put up with the rough draft of everything

TABLE OF CONTENTS

TESTIFY

Seeing Aunt Sister

THE BIG SHOW

This poem begins at 4 pm, in front of the TV,
on a green rug, edited for time. It is a Tuesday,
so even joy will have consequences. Friday,
and this poem might crush Tokyo or be doomed
to drink your blood. Wednesday, comic; Monday,
a mystery; Thursday, romance with song & dance.

This poem might have been fun with giant ants
in tap shoes. Or werewolves. What if the love
story took place onstage, not in teary flashbacks?
There might be a murder. Color. Bar fights. But
this poem begins at 4 pm Tuesday. You know
that accepting any premise has consequences.

She Is Like a Mary Sue

It has been asked
who is she & what
is her infinitive, and that's a good question.

You might say:

like God, Aunt Sister
is a Mary Sue,
a disco ball winking
back your own eye.

Or. Photo filter, opalescent light bulb—
she dissolves your blemishes
with her flattering glow.

She was created to die.

But also: to love, to grieve,
to wake
        (as if the sleeping beauty—her
        castle about to be demolished—
        had been relocated)

confused but treasured &

        loved as one should love one's best self.

Four Clear Words in a Whispered Room

She was lying with her back toward absence,
night after night. Survivor on a wreck of long days,
she saw "Solstice" on the calendar, opened
the windows and doors and washed her home
to the skin then sagged exhausted.

It was not wholly dark, summer dusk,
but the cherrywood bed was taut
with sun-stiff sheets and blue drunkard's path.
The dressed pillows were set aside to sit
like a man in the chair. She surrendered.
                                    Entire and flat-backed,
a spread woman, an X, she slept the clock around.
Morning was evening's clone, or might have been.

Years later, in a muted public room, four words
she understood as "this is called prayer" reminded her
—somehow—of this. A fortune cookie message,
the words didn't change a thing, yet she was pleased
to rest on the puzzle of their context.

She Is Born in the Rain

The woman who had not yet been born had been riding
the winding local Trailways bus all morning and into

afternoon. Her station was nowhere, a gray limestone
slurry in front of an anonymous store, the world.

The driver drew her suitcase from the belly of the bus
and set it beside her left loafer. Brown shoes and leather-

handled suitcase darkened, rainspot by spot. She was
a winter tree, a sick dog, blown sheet of newsprint

about to tear. Then the store behind her opened,
and warm air blew her old name off and away, over

the soggy fields, and into a tree with a bird's sorry nest.
Five people talking at once might have been hundreds,

for all the sense they made. One of them, a little girl,
tugged to get her attention and called her Aunt Sister.

That silly name made the sun come out; she kept it.

Rubies in the Gravel

To have been loved
                        is a star on the point of the moon.

Suppose you mis-step, stumble on a rolling pebble:
you may lose sight of something rare
but may discover a ruby in the gravel.

What if, at ten, she had not tripped, split her lip,
scarred her mouth? That was a crumb
he wanted to lick away
the first time he saw her.

What if some other man
had touched her shoulder—that way—first.
What if Tom hadn't been a fool, or Mike

a little kinder. What if she'd missed meeting Frank.
What if the rain, the sun, if Frank had refused to die.

She came to the family bereft
and archaic: Ruth,
cherry petals and snow, a lovely city shocked by bombs.

What if she had come sure-footed, needing no one,
her grief whistled into a yellow taxi?
She could have gone away, left them undiscovered.

To have been loved
is the star, and seeing the star.
To have been loved is a pebble underfoot.

Birds in a Sentimental Movie

Is there a word for the yoke of crescents, shorthand
enacting a bird flying away to the distance?

***

She is the bird in that sentimental movie, a broad
with a heart, whip-smart dialog and feathered mules.

***

She is an Art Deco stateroom; canary in satin
with maid, complications, and full orchestra.

***

She is Jenny Wren. Or Tweety. Minerva's owl
or maybe Minerva. She is a hummingbird. Crow.

***

Born in the rain and remembered like a song,
she was hatched to fly, rest, delight and depart.

***

There is no reason for a hawk or mockingbird.
There is no reason for a woman, dragon, flamingo.

COUSIN JILL

I like a woman who can fall
Jack said to Jill.
But Jill, who had some Gatewelder blood,
knew there would be bruises,
and tears to mend,
and a dented bucket to find and fill
and explanations to make
again. There always were.
And if I don't get out of here,
she told her diary that night, that hill
that bucket and that man
will re-enact me to my grave,
I know they will.

CYNTHIA

My father-in-law tells me: All
Gatewelders are strong. Honey, now you're family,
and you're strong, too.
      And he wants that to be true. But can't
say the words to my face, between baldness
and parts that can't be mended with patience,
dowels, and glue. So he talks toward the river
and the round hill beyond my shoulder, saying
to them you know we love you. You be strong.

CONSTANCE

Constance
is an easy sleeper,
but some nights her bladder wakes her
and Nathan tosses and snores. So she walks
down the hall in the dark past the pictures she knows,
through dining room, living room, back again.
White, in her night gown, a ghost. She talks
in a whisper to infants who've grown away,
now parents with babies to walk back to sleep.

A Gatewelder Story

Sliced tomatoes on the table, red to the core, big
as a big man's fist; mashed new potatoes, bowl
of pepper gravy; sweet corn, on the cob and fried;
green beans with ham hock; baby onion peas;
field peas; light bread; cornbread; new peach preserves;
jam cake…and apple fried pies. Where's the chicken,
says Sam. Everybody hushes. And Sam sits there,
doesn't touch a thing, even his tea. Waiting for meat.

Doris is with Mama in the kitchen, new to the family. Shy.
And nobody knows her either or has seen her mad. Yet.
Even she sees Sam would rather shame Mama than eat,
would rather have his own way than own the moon.
And Mama's halfway to frying him some ham. Doris
stops washing and comes out, big knife in her hand.
She takes an egg from the blue bowl on the sideboard,
and cracks it on his head. Says: You want gravy
with that chicken?

They got to be friends later, more or less. Sam
said he'd have them put that on her tombstone.

She Was Stunned Dull/Breaking Alive

It is not enough to exist (you must live), and ecstasy
had become a strange religious memory,

a lightspoke that once upon a time pierced
infinite grays. Stunned dull, she had grieved.

Tea from a thin bag, old in the pantry. White saltines
with cardboard swiss, dull surrender of a mealy apple.

Thinking she had lost her sense of smell and flavors
because it was too difficult to be alive,

she still smiled for others. Walked where they directed,
nodded in time to the chat and rumble, squinted

into the afternoon glare off tin roof and glass.
One of the women pinched the tip leaves off a plant. Smell!

And the world broke her alive again in peppermint.

she never formulated an answer.
Never cast her reasons
into silver charms. His ponderous joy and gallantry.
His eyes—deep and swimming green—
suggesting underwater kingdoms
or rainbow trout. His practicality and failure not
to see Tom Sawyer in his mirror.

ELEVEN LETTERS FROM FRANK

1.
I am traveling away now,
with your breath still in my lungs; my hands
are nothing but your smell.

2.
There is no place to be alone.
I want to touch
where you touched.

3.
I have a vision of the two of us, old
and covered with grandkids. Two
facing pages covered with letters.

4.
How do you do it?
While I sleep, you hover over me.
The air is still warm (from you) when I wake up.

5.
When I see you again, I will crush
you into my chest.
No more separations.

6.
You inhabit my pocket.
Silver, wicked, flint and wheel.
You are my torch, my campfire, girl.

7.
I left you. I blame you.
Crazy. I'm blazing and chills.
I dream you as the ocean.

8.
Bleak rock and gray water, gray clouds.
Gray gulls sit on the wind.
Cold as a mortuary slab.

9.
How can you be so quickly nebulous?
What color are you wearing?
Open a Coke and drink it so I can taste you.

10.
When I get back we'll play
our love scene fifty times, and no
director shouting cut, cut, cut.

11.
There's a bird I've heard every night for a week.
One opaque song
against the transparent world.

THE CONDENSED VERSION

She's like Noah.
Has a temper, and a saw:
makes angry boats.

She's a teacher.
Waves her hands
like rain on thirsty trees.

When she's walking, poems
follow her like rabbit hounds
or hickory smoke.

She's a phenomenon.
Nobody knows her mind.
She's diagrammed like a hurricane.

She hears voices,
and they won't shut up.
They love her.

Someday she'll die;
that won't upset the wind,
and she'll be gone.

ONE UNDERGOES THE CHANGE

Change separates reality from fiction. Even God
changes the socks he wears in public (lest humans
auto-destruct at the sight of his Awesome Feet).

Frank's widow finished school. Added
degrees, became a teacher and scholar.
Traveled to Europe (England twice, Denmark),
spent a fine October spring in Perth,
was silent for a month in Alabama.

She had some friends who were lovers;
some lovers became friends; some,
did not. She swam twice weekly at the Y,
sang Hallelujah every Christmas, took one
boxing lesson. She grew a little stout (her word)
and a little more than gray, had moles removed
(benign), and bought pretty perfume
blended to her post-menopausal scent.
                                    One night
that woman woke from the middle of a nightmare, sure
she was having a heart attack and dying, and was right.
Our protagonist, however, is only a fiction and continues
unabated.

ONE OF THE COUSINS CALLS ON HIS WIDOWED AUNT

Whatever God is—worship, understanding,
and belief belong in the pockets of our messy flesh.

Flesh, with a black suitcase from Walmart,
has arrived, uninvited, by bus and his first ever taxi,

and stands at the doorstep of his last hope and illusion.
He rings the doorbell. From the playground he passed

a block and a half ago come two uninflected shrieks
like a red and white plastic whistle, and he jumps

a little. Waiting on the doorstep was not in his
scenario. Two white cabbage butterflies, a mockingbird.

A helicopter passes the corner church, just higher
than steeple and maples. The pressure in his ears.

Sound beats against his chest and the opening door
is a silent movie.

A Niece Sleeps on the Sofa Bed

To see yourself in someone else's dream
is like an autopsy. Once

while she was a student, she remembers:
we went to the morgue, a weak-kneed gaggle
in shapeless paper gowns, masks, deflated balloon
hats. With balloons over our shoes. (Afraid
we'd carry death home in our insoles.) The woman
on the table would have laughed
if she had been around, but laughter was long gone.
Nothing left but nakedness.

In her niece's dream, stripped
of anything but metaphor, she
was preternaturally tall, a dress on stilts.
But her makeup was perfect, and her eyes kind.

She Dreams of Her Husband Frank

Not too many weeks or months or years
(time was running together) before she died

the woman who was not exotic, warm, happy,
and embraced with round-armed love

—that woman had a dream she thought
upon waking had been her dead husband.

She was in a hollow space, glassed crosswalk
between wings of some building. With rain

splattering the world and a din. There had been something
in her hand. A ball of rubber bands? Maybe Tinkerbell.

Nothing to do with Frank. Yet Frank—
whose face she no longer remembers, only photograph-Frank—

was an object in her hand. Now she is stuffy
from crying. Sounds of receding thunder. And the young man

with whom she had been married is still frozen in his frame
on the dresser. She supposes he would understand how, often,

when he appears in her dreams someone she knows
now must point him out.

SEEING AUNT SISTER

How long had it been? No one could remember.
She missed Christmas, but with some good excuse,
and the big October birthday celebration. She'd been scarce
in September, August, May. How long? One of Sarah's boys
said he'd run into her last spring up at Gethsemane.
They sat, talked about Merton, the weather, and crows
until vesper bells called the monks to prayer.
The last thing he remembered her saying was odd,
but like her. A quote that jumbled locks
and keys with hawks and cell biology. He guessed
she might have looked a little tired.

The hospice nurse spoke for her eroded body:
ventriloquist and doll. He rounded out
the language of her plucks and sighs,
and talked until her strength waned. She dozed.
The family stayed. Caught up on children,
cars, dogs, meetings, separations. Together,
they watched gray distant clouds draw rain shades
across the farthest hills and the near ones.
And watched the vegetation by the window
quiver with some scattered drops and darken.

THE WOMAN'S BODY OVER TIME

This is a photograph of the woman's body over time.
There, where she is younger, she is a river
with a river's arms. Fish tickle the small pool of her back.
Her breasts are sun-scaled. Matured she is, as seen
here, a gently used automobile. Glossy,
chrome on all four wheels, she has treated herself
to high-end upholstery and steam-cleaned
her engine compartment. She taught her chassis
to belly dance, spritzes her hair with that new hair smell. She died,
and became separate elements—a yarrow stick or two,
the hanged man, a magic eight ball. Now the women
of the family call out readings of her moods
based on the scent of room she left
a moment before they entered.

Bad Knees

The Woman with Bad Knees
and the Baleen Whale

The woman with bad knees
winced her way to the window.
She needed inspiration.
She was having a hard time.
There was no room in her poem
for a red biplane. But it was necessary:
its cartoon engine made the putt-putts
that tickled her mind.

Out the window, in the wide world,
were pepper grains of people.
Trees, and small teardrop trucks, would
fit into her poem, but not a plane
with cartoon putts.

The woman wished with her heart,
her eyes, and aching knees
for the great baleen of inspiration to rise
from the pavement like a globe of silver bubbles.
Its krill syllables hanging on a pause,
it would drink her poem and exhale

a red biplane.

Compulsion

when it comes over her
what she would not do

just to make it go away
just to get a little peace

ask a junkie why he fills his veins
when it comes over her

ask her why do you write junk
why not say something

about your passion
what she would not do

for a good passion
for God or sunsets or stamps

but her need is her passion
just to make it go away

what she wants is a subject
some butter pecan helps

just not for long
just to get a little peace

she pairs columns A and B
she adds her laundry and some salt

when it comes over her
that's what she does

THE WOMAN WITH BAD KNEES RETURNS

She had been driving through green hills for hours,
and home was so near now that she knew
it was impossible to reach. Her eyes burned.

When she opened the car door,
her feet in their pink plastic sandals
seemed foreign to the parking lot.

Salma Hayek, smiling, was checking an elderly couple
into the hotel. That the woman thought them elderly,
her peers, was a measure of her exhaustion.

That she saw them as a couple, when their bodies
were one nimbus of lavender stars, she only thought odd.
The desk clerk also seemed blurred,

and the woman wondered, for a moment,
how a halo had come by Ms. Hayek's beautiful face.
Outside the picture window, paused

to watch the sun set, Antonio Banderas
was watering the flowers, pink begonias. The woman
sought her room. By the ice machine, an Asian

Antonio Banderas was lighting a furtive cigarette.
While she struggled with the red-green signals
of the locked door —slow, no —fast, yes! A Norwegian

Salma and Antonio, but with accents from the woman's
home, were returning from the pool, trailed
by child versions of their glowing

selves, with towels. Inside the room, the face
above the white sink belonged to the aching
woman. Its eyes were tired of beauty.

Closing Time, Home

Time of sour bar towels and sudden owls,
pocket change on the dresser, a comb.

Next door the band rolls in from Amy's,
high, unloads moody rhythms and chords.

I have a dream with Richard Widmark, not
young or in his prime, just this old man

singing karaoke. The lounge walls
are carved like stelae, painted tan, red,

storm-blue. The barman chants out: Closing
time. I don't care where you go. Irene,

good-night. Widmark blinks out. I'm alone;
the moon is where the moon should be. If

this were Nashville ars poetic, hymns
would underlie the hour like owl amens.

What's Put Away

It isn't just drunk fools
who howl at the moon or bluesmen
and boys with their hearts
between their legs. Women moan,
and girls who don't know why. Tell you a secret:

When I was young—eleven
or ten—I cut the dirty words out of my mother's dictionary.
Cut them with big, black kitchen shears. It was hard:
the paper was thin and each page had two columns,
like the Bible. Words, pronunciations, definitions;
slivers, translucent below their ink;
all things genital, secondary, scatalogical
I stuffed into a dimestore white envelope, hid
in a hollow tree on Hogan Road.

WHAT SHE WANTS

The mouth of a tarnished trumpet tastes like nickels and dimes
and is not a piano. *She's seven: she doesn't know
what she wants.* I didn't want worn-out nickels and dimes,
a case with thin velvet like corduroy knees. I closed that away.

One night, a bar, a guy.
We went to his house to get high.
He poured cheap wine; his roommate rolled cheap weed.
They talked. Talked. They talked and I was bored, and went
exploring. In a bedroom found, somehow fixed to the wall,

the guts of a small piano, fully strung. I stroked the strings,
and it purred. From a bench before it, I tap-danced its wires
with gray felt hammers. I made music like buckets, and keys;
like rocks and fingers, sex in river fog; like Underwood uprights,
foot-wide stairstep limestone creeks; like shining silver horns.
It sounded my mind, tasted like cherries flambé.

When You Need Them

Kid. Lives with her grandmother.
Wears a stupid hat.
All the time. Fuzzy hat.
Nasty.
Looks like a dead dog.
One day
her grandmother says
your daddy and his girlfriend
are coming this afternoon
to pick you up
and take you away.
Kid says
no damn way. Don't
swear, Grandma says.
You go hide in the
shed out back. I'll
lie. Say you ran off.
Kid says don't lie.
The devil will get you.
Anyway, that's them
out in the driveway. Kid
says I'll be back by
supper, opens the door.
Granny goes to the kitchen.

Soak the chicken
in buttermilk, bake a little
cake. There never
are any fairies.

The Wrong Fairy Tale

You step into some room
      for the first time
      and know, from subtle cues
      —a slinking shape
      or no smell of gingerbread
           —that you've opened
the wrong fairy tale.

This isn't the pom-pom poodle edition,
cardboard corners
rubbed fluffy,
porcelain doll in a red cape
split-oak basket on her arm,
      and that pressed and pristine white napkin.

This is hardcore noir
      in a rust-black pickup,
           crouched by a late-night grocery.
Too far from the entrance,
      too close to your path;
           shadows hide the watcher.
You won't like how this will end.

The Woman with Bad Knees, and Magic

The woman with bad knees knows the mirage
of magic beans. They take too long, she insists.
Not meaning the overnight sprout cloudward.
It is the climb she knows to be impossible.
And besides, magic beans cannot exist. She
is sensible. Sane as grass around autumn crocus.

But in the stillness of her heart below her fears,
and in the secret marrow of her massive hips,
spells want to unfold their saffron-centered recipes
like pleated windows. Hand over your stock
of well-magicked beans—and get out of her way.

Be they pintos with neon flowers, pearl moon
sweet peas, or limas virus-etched with Adam
and the god in microscopic splendor twenty-four
crayolas bright—she will pop joints and clatter
to the back of the garage where she last saw
the trowel. And not once pause for breath
until that magic's in the ground and watered.

CHAS. BUKOWSKI WORKS

This is the way I imagine it. Charles
Bukowski is still writing. He's sitting
on the floor of his hotel. Called the Great
Eternal Flophouse, it is both heaven
and hell. Which, depends on the plumbing
on any particular floor. Bukowski's
room has a wash basin and a closet-
sized space with a toilet and tin shower
but no door. That doesn't matter: no one
visits. The bed with its sagging springs sees
no action. There's a dresser in the room,
with a blank frame where its mirror hasn't
been replaced. An eternally dusty
faded red armchair waits by the window.
Bukowski sits on the bare wood floor,
his back against the wall, with a yellow
legal pad and a new yellow pencil.
Half a pack of cigarettes and a souvenir
ashtray in the shape of a sombrero.
Bottle and glass. Because it's Labor Day—
the American version of May Day—
Bukowski, like Whitman down the hall, like
dos Pasos and Steinbeck and Hemingway,
Dorothy Parker—it's a big goddamn
flophouse and I could go on—is writing
to honor the American working
man (and woman). The floor hasn't been mopped
in three months of Sundays. The housekeeper
slipped on a broken step and shattered her
right kneecap. Surgeon who fixed it said
the pieces reminded him of a wooden
puzzle map of the Lower Forty-Eight
he used to love when he was a kid.

Bukowski's brain is on fire. All the words
pertaining to the great American
worker are up there like sheep in a pen.
To be their shepherd, he thinks, is good work.

AFTER PABLO

What were you following when I followed you
at the end of *Il Postino*? What tugged you
through the paired lobby doors, past the ticket booth,
and on, to the sidewalk so abruptly Nashville?

I wanted to learn more from you, about life,
and the night. Or maybe only about poetry. What
were you peering after in the darkness?
And how is it that you never tripped? Even though
the sidewalk heaves and wobbles
from high-rooted sycamores, your silhouette
never stumbled any more than a cat would falter,
or a hunting hound.

You didn't climb the steep plank ramp at Savarino's,
or I would have gone there, too, bought you an espresso,
and if you wanted, the pale Italian cookies
with flecks of sun, *tarallucci al limone*. But no,
you passed on the opposite sidewalk.

You visited no one that night. You could have knocked
on any door. I once knew an artist on that street
of stained bricks, coal dust from forgotten furnaces
blending the bungalows together. My friend
would have opened his door with pleasure for you.

I lost you among hackberry trees. In the grove
by the dragon park. The shade of you blended with theirs
and you disappeared as I watched. A small black dog
emerged sniffing and wagging from the shadows
and picnic tables to keep me company
while I waited until the sun rose.

What did you find? What did you learn?
On the way home I bought a day-old pastry
and broke off crusty bites for the dog, grateful
for his company. When I opened my front door,
he trotted off, pausing now and then
to inspect a cigarette butt in the gutter,
a drift of fallen sycamore balls.

THE ISLAND

Kristin-who-cuts-my-hair describes her long-
postponed honeymoon in the Bahamas. She

Snip says it was a telephone offer. Who
in their right mind would? But they did.

In the mirror, behind blue Barbicide,
she shapes thin sheets of hair as she talks.

But she's only a blur—her island grows, sweet
and luxurious, through my reflection. Later, home,

and the Weather shows a swirling egg yolk,
red as a dragon's eye, aimed at the Bahamas.

Someone told me once: Don't go to Paris,
it's not there. And if you loved the book,

don't see the movie, ever. Untroubled by storms,
Kristin's green lizards smile on from pink walls.

A Miser's Life

The trees in the Art Center courtyard are small,
an October grove of adolescent elms.
Their stiff leather oval-round leaves turned
yellow overnight and fell the next night
onto the white gravel. And the wind heaped them
beside the walk, and I had just arrived
when the damn sun suddenly struck coins, right
before my eyes. I had to set my purse down,
had to bend and scoop a double handful.
If the leaves were nasty underneath with damp,
dead bugs and cigarette butts, it really
didn't matter. They fell through my fingers,
and I was Scrooge McDuck, living large
in a top hat, my hands dripping gold.

Barefoot Madrigal

My bare feet soak up the sun: two old white cats
on the porch in the morning. This is spring. It's home
and it's a mystery, deep as your bones.

A pair of squirrels spirals down the pine, batty
as hell. Under my soles, the concrete's warm;
my bare feet soak up the sun: two old white cats
on the porch in the morning. This is spring. It's home.

And warm light twirls a buzzard like a hat
in blue that's lush, and deep enough to drown
you. Nothing's finished yet, life's just turning.
My bare feet soak up the sun: two old white cats
on the porch in the morning. This is spring. It's home
and it's a mystery, deep as your bones.

WHEN SHE WAS VENUS

One day,
a nesting-doll of books and dogs
    and rock-and-roll; pimento cheese,
        dreams, rum, text messages, and humdrum
  in a shell of shapeless day-to-day straightened her back
while the whine of the vacuum shuddered off.
    The dense hush expected another unremarkable chore
      and everything was waiting
when the TV in the other room began to sing. "Speak low,"
advised its song, "when you speak love."
    Strings rose behind the words wind-warm,
      found a space among the woman's nestled layers
  empty as a night between two days,
    fit there like a lacquer skin.
And she was on the beach,
    feet bare; and the damp cooling sand stretched flat
      between a bonfire and the moon, she
a dancer,
    her back to the partner who lifted her
      as a wave lifts foam or a fire its light.

How could she have forgotten?
    She smiled, amazed. And later that day
      smiled again
        for no reason.
    And the next.
Speak low.

FROM THE GOSPEL ACCORDING TO THE WOMEN WITH TWO FIRST NAMES

And on that day
we were asking Jesus
—*why do you say she is pretty?*

meaning, of course,
—we
play by the rules, pay our daily
sacrifice and, because it's what's expected, pirouette
before the crowd and absorb all kinds of
ridicule, humiliation, etc.

meaning
—we are deeply hurt, lord
—aren't we pretty, too?
And, lo, he did say unto us women,

woman woman woman
it is obvious
y'all are caught up, caught up from birth,
every single one, in wanting
external validation,
bless your hearts.
Watch:

And he did one of his good-housekeeping miracles
changing oil and water into an emulsion
or darkness into star-spangled
when what we wanted
was to be called pretty.

We don't ask for parables.
We can get those from the locusts
and the orange-eyed cicadas, sermoning
at their aircraft-engine decibels
as if being loud made them more worthwhile.
We want the bone translation,
tongue truth,
want to know in our blood
the trembling of it
evermore.

Tell us we're pretty, too.

BIPLANE OVER THE KOKOSING VALLEY

One noon moment, I was a red biplane,
tilted between round hills and river trees:
a kite, a cherry, a breath in a line.
The paused red float that validates cane
pole dozing, I floated over rows of green
that blue noon when I was a red biplane.
What else could teach me what I had to learn?
The art to shim dense words or squeeze
a kite, a cherry, and a breathing line
into a dip-glazed sky, so smoothly plain
it must have a hawk or buzzard. Or me,
being for that moment a red biplane
juggling bits of sixty-four years, this time
without sputtering. Now I may claim these:
a kite, a cherry, a breath in a line
like a buzzard bending blue. These are mine
to leaven with, sweeten with, use. Because
one noon moment I was a red biplane,
a kite, a cherry, a breath in a line.

FIG

Her man. She licks his back, a cat, a breeze. Work in the sun,
he returns delicious with rolling sweat, a ripe fig fragrant to her teeth.

Younger than an egg, the wind kicks the springy branches
just a hiccup. Without the tree, there'd be nothing to detect.

Who can translate the wind in the fig?
There's a wren nesting behind one green, unwritten page.

Bird and tree. One leaves in spring, one in fall. It is summer,
and they have come together like rest and a good conscience.

Teacher sat in the cluster of fig limbs, a rabbit, dozing.
All day the infant wind hummed the same green-purple note.

When the old woman was sick, we almost murdered the fig tree for fans.
That was not our first mistake, but we and the fig are still friends.

Drink/Word

I have grown
up, out, and old

drinking invisible tea,
diving blind-to-the-world

into paper vats of whiskey
cadences. Syntax spoken

by no known race curls
around my throat, beads,

penetrates my tongue—
layers deeper than mother

words. I have played
patty-cake with gods

and named dragons. How
can such weird power

buy noodle soup,
answer email?

How the Universe Is Like Passionflowers

If I can use a word in a sentence,
the thing so named exists. Maybe
not enough to bless your daily bread,
or to rampage with a chain saw.

A branch weighing hundreds of pounds falls.
Two people meet. Someone wants lemons
for iced tea, and hurries to the store. How many times
have I not died? And you—how many? If the best man
had not pranked the condoms, what?

Hold this in your off hand while you review the universe:
probability's a ruse. The first and the ninety-second
flip of the quarter, six of one to half a dozen: tails.
The passionflower is wild and strange;
its sweet fruit gives you dreams.

Pasture rose; painted trillium; the freckled,
blushing pitcher plant, a carnivore; around the woods
that skirt of mayapple umbrellas; muscadines;
persistent human souls. That life exists elsewhere
and that it doesn't are both improbable.

How can anything so common as a honeysuckle
make you drunk and nostalgic? When we bought the house,
one corner of chain link fence belonged to gold and ivory.
It was summer—imagine the smell as afternoon began to cool—
and suddenly, all that was something I owned.

That I could be adult, responsible, grow heirloom tomatoes—
is about as likely as a passionflower vining
through chains and honeysuckle. So improbable,
that flower. That I write a poem. That it's read.

ONTOLOGY

This is my house, this box on paper painted
khaki cream. Black slapdash strokes
are windows on its sides. In front—
another window, and a door (to which we shall return).
The back was meant to be plain but, well, I painted
a garden on its wall. Daisies, mostly,
and asters, zinnias. (Not good with peony, larkspur,
love-in-a-mist complications. I suggest them with splats.)
Larger than any flower, a bee sports, black and yellow acrylic.
So. House, garden, windows. A door that doesn't open.

Once, I bought a Home Depot hollow-core door.
Placed across two file cabinets,
it became my desk. What if I should cut along the lines
of my paper home's door, remove the rectangle,
leave it leaning, maybe against a flower, and a gust
sends it fluttering and sliding along sidewalk and street—
then drops it to lie face-down in the intersection. Cars,
UPS trucks, couples with strollers roll over it, making patterns.
Pebbles dimple the paper. Is it a door?

Meanwhile, empty space remains
by the solitary front window.
Enter the box by way of that space, and it is
a portal, a passage, a doorway: a door.
I can't lock the wolf out, or my painted kitten, in.
It has no hinges and no knob, can't be placed across two files
to be a desk. And yet—

)

SWINGING BRIDGE

This is my bewilderment: a straight line.
This is my puzzlement.
Horses and the opal are secrets. God, an obfuscation. How is it

that the plank of an arched bridge is straight,
when each hair of your sardonic brow
bows like a leaf? How

is it possible: the oyster
and the pearl?

The bone at the base of the spine is called sacred;
a waterlily grows from muck. That throat
whose vibrations sing lullaby,

swallowed blackened redfish. How
can truth and lie both hold kindness? A boat keeps out
what a bucket contains. A lake surface scattering light

and its clear, if fishy, interior are the same.
This is my riddle. A line of verse,
straight as a board, has all of heaven in it, swaying.

Testify

the blackbird said
it was dark inside
and smelled of fire and lard
too tightly packed to move
they pretended it was night
inside the casket of crust
the knife that freed them passed
between two feathers of his wing
and damaged one barb
there was noise then
brightness and confusion
I asked him did you sing
we escaped, he said
we did not sing

BLUES FOR THE FISHERMAN

Since the blues ought to be tall birds
wading and wailing
when the sun dies—
let the blues fill its lungs now:

the hard-working sun dips
and folds into the hills and rocks,
and the stars begin to show up
one one.

As the sun dies, love it with the blues.

When a man dies
hurt ought to be a monsoon
moaning denial. When a man dies—
do despise that peacock sunset,

despise the ping ping emergence of stars,
drown their fluty condolence, damp their trills.
When a man dies
let grief swallow the light

and the heron in twilight.

[In fact I was not there]

In fact I was not there
but I seem to be standing in the dining room,
where Daddy would serve us his Thanksgivings.
I am holding the receiver of the heavy black phone
in that alcove crowded with brown veneer
and look like someone who is listening with comprehension.

Or maybe I did go home
while the coroner talked on,
even after father became body.

LAMENTATION

I am a grief a guilt
I am a diet
of dyers' herbs
woad and madder
a suite of lamentations
made from drought and thorns
as chapters made from words
nihil
like a dog
like a dog with sore feet, and burrs
I emphasize pain
howling from my raw
nihil
nihil
nothing and dire
hopeless straits and hollow marrow
no mercy on the starving and the dust
mercy no mercy on the cattle drowning
silent frogs and still tadpoles nihil
the broken cities the greedy streets
our houses framed with dead men's bones
we have stolen the twigs out of cook fires
stolen the very water from the pot
the kerosene from lanterns
how can we not play brass laments
for fishermen's poisoned pools
black crawfish, and fouled rice
how can we not march slow
for the murdered mothers
daughters and sons
our gates are beautiful locked
hold nothing
hold nothing at bay
nihil and I am sorry sorry
words change nothing
and are bitter in the mouth

The Nature of Time and a Story

Before the woman died, there was no future without her.
Thus we learn that the future also comes from nothing.

Once I heard a good story. Whether it was Crow told it,
my iron kettle, or the dull black checker I keep

that belonged to my grandfather, I can't recall. But:
used to be there was no time, and everything was and will be

all at once. People were. Never existed. Saw things beyond
comprehension every day. Every day happened and didn't

and would and shouldn't. Every day. Even breathing
was a confusion of whether to inhale. Back then,

although history was everywhere it hadn't been invented.
Who was it invented time and history? Who shook out the kinks,

sprinkled on water, and put a hot iron to existence? Who
flattened the past with starch and made the future steam?

Crow would have said it was the bird clan. Kettle,
that time was a man-made thing. My dull black checker

would say time was a lie my grandfather told to keep me quiet.
I can't say. All three stories are in my mind like truth. Of course,

the woman is in my mind, too, and she's dead and been dead.

Time Is a Desert of Rain

Again the wind
and the gray-toned clouds.
Again the sun
is a broad, bright moon.
Again I ache,
bruised from winter years.

I forget why
spring disappoints me.

If the body creates tribes of cells
charged to manufacture joy,
mine have become nomads,
following rumors of light. When
did they last know a home? A porch.
A place to sit and knit elation
while the long rains fall.

MAYFLY

1.
When the mayflies appear, they must seem to the fish
like manna, God's undeserved bounty wasted
onto the water's skin. As if they could not get enough
by grazing, fish will rise like light off the ripples
to catch mayflies still in the air.

2.
The grandfather I remember was senile. White hair.
Toothless as a moth. He wore bib overalls and plaid flannel
or white cotton shirts. He scowled, said nothing not
a growl or mumble, ate cornbread souped in buttermilk
with a tea spoon from a tall jelly glass.

3.
I was small, playing Chinese Checkers with my grandmother,
diamond board like a Lone Star quilt; it was summer.
My grandfather came into the room and picked up a cane-
bottom chair like a fly swatter, waving it. My grandmother
stepped between us, a round matador. I've forgotten the rest.

4.
When he was gone at last and his body lay, stern
in a new suit in the guest bedroom, family and neighbors
came to the farm, waited awake through the night. Women
in straight chairs were an oval orbit spun out from the hickory fire.
Men with cigarettes in the late fall darkness were crickets of light.

5.
A day may come to represent a class of days,
specimens of natural history. A dragonfly with isinglass wings,
transparent as the bladder of a fish, could stand as a mayfly
or damsel. One woman: many. A long shape in the water might
be a garfish, body, log. Even clear, untroubled—time distorts.

MONSTER

She explained that she suffered under a curse.
That she had been a pumpkin before. She recounted
a lifetime of sunshine. Rain was ecstasy beyond
her powers of speech: she might have been a saint of rain.
The magician who made her first a golden coach,
and then a woman, was the devil of her cosmology,
having forced form, fate and function on a soul
that wanted nothing but to ripen, rot,
fulfill a simple mandate, without
all of this talking.

GEOMETRY OF THE VANISHING POINT

white August grasses, bone January leaves:
their scent

the grain of your voice and pauses,
followed across the sill of sleep

sunset
occurring within a storm

cessation of pain

Absence began with a stutter-step,
became a rift, a cliff, a flight from
which Mom would return, baffled,
and sad for the bones of her arms.
When the weather let him, he would
walk his mother to the lake beyond
the parking lot. He pushed the chair
like a shopping cart, said Look, Mom,
a goldfinch. Said mallard. Cattails.
Said I was rereading the Mahfouz
you gave me and thought. Said
clouds, cumulus. Nourishing words
to sustain a dying language. Once
they found her, resting, on a green
rickety park bench. I was going to
the store for bread and that soda
my boy likes. Thank you.
I have been longing for a cup of tea.

TESTIFY

The mother of your soul died
aged, and beautiful to you as cedar
or black bamboo. You prayed then
in your own way, letter by letter,
a tear knotted into every syllable.
And I envy you her and her, you.
Grass in a busted flower pot envying
a limestone glade. Some days I'm so dry
the future is too brittle and thin
to trust, and the past has worn itself
featureless, flat as paper. It's then
I wish for a sign painter of the old,
migrant, alcoholic kind. To make my walls
say something clear. Like EATS, or GOD,
and beautifully, even if it is a lie.

JUSTICE

All their spites, enmity
are rocks she picks up—volunteer
clearing landmines, sanitation
engineer, nurse, connoisseur
of hatred. Her hands full
of knife-edged obsidian and blunt
time-honored slurs, she hugs
them to her chest, holds them
in her mouth, bleeds. What
she can't hold, she swallows.
I said: Don't hold that grudge.
It will only cripple you. She
dropped it on my foot.

Pain

Why
am I not raging?
Why aren't we all?
All so flaming angry
we burn our shoes. Heaps of shoes
should burn
at intersections,
and when the flames begin to flag
why are we not angry enough
to feed the fire with bread
and cans of tuna in oil.
Feed the conflagration
olive oil and coffee
and Ikea shelving units.
We have broken the camel
with all of our straws:
why are we not
all rage, skinless
boneless, dripping.
Why doesn't it hurt so
that we slit
our dogs' throats
and our cats'. Throw
beloved carcasses on the pyre,
park our Toyotas around it
and Transport Vans
and open their doors to spill
Jane Austen, treasured photos,
footballs, our grandmothers'
watches each
with two
diamond chips, spill ourselves
into the consumption.

I Never Dreamed I'd Be This Old

Through the blue insoles of my supportive shoes,
the heat pump's vibration enters my bones.
My heels are humming, my shins, and knees. Tuesday
augurs to rock me like a xylophone.

The first crow flying over barks five times.
Three trail behind him, puffs of black smoke
against the blue. Below the ridge a train
whines freight eastward behind four locomotives.

Halfway through November and leaves still cling
like light to the big oaks down the fence row.
The bald cypress trees are red as foxes;
I am spectacular, too. As I sing
through the dishes and the dusting, I grow
too light to count my own paradoxes.

PRAYER TO A SHEET-METAL SAINT IN INDIANA

I want to sleep. Sleep twenty dreams. More.
A thousand. And wake up still holding all
the words and the order. Recreate me
a savant of sleep, to recall my soul
woven through twenty fiddle tunes, fifty
tickets around the carousel, every tall
tale and lie men tell. Float me and drift me
beyond daily mazes and mundane walls.

I want to sleep late. Taste every flower
in the honeycomb, make my every shot.
Deal me a free pass, craft me a charm
of access to the treble-barred tower.
Treat me to a hammock, spread me a cot.
To lie all day like a breath, what's the harm?

THIS BODY

This body aches in its joints and connections
because I have forgotten it. I have forgotten,
for weeks on end: to breathe. For months:
to release my hands. This spine is confused
if I turn. Habituated to wall horizons,
these eyes fail against the planes of windows.

Winter settled me into myself, left food
and fluffy slippers—and went on its way. So.

I drowse through humming rooms, check the mail,
drive in a dream to fetch more cereal.
In this hypnagogic state only imagine
opening doors, windows, throwing wide my arms
and taking in gelid winter air like opium—
body comfort, particular as pain.

NINE-AND-SIXTY

An old woman in a cracked house loves equally
the goldfinch upside down at thistle on the porch
and the yellow-breasted backhoe that chugs akimbo,
puffs, and dips beak into the neighbors' trench.
The woman is considering her last will and testament.
Rather, say: ought to be, but is avoiding it.
grasshopper, grasshopper, never learned

If one train leaves for Memphis going west at 8 am
and four men dig a 40-foot well in 4 days, how long
is one compound life minus one? What if the hand you always
grab, to pull yourself up out of ditches, is gone?
Into the gray beginnings of morning, she washes things;
in blue pajamas, windowpanes. Put grieving aside, aside, aside
there's the electric, and medicines, gas for the car.
Cranky old woman found dead in her home. Leaving cats…
not yet, grasshopper, finish your chores

A woman with no will or testament, gray raincoat
over her pajamas, on the front porch in the morning
refills a plastic cylinder with thistle. Finches are wasteful.
Black ants in a line cart their leftovers away. It's too late
to become ant-like. Sturdy. A banker of seeds and success.
She feeds the cats. Because she can't go starting
over. And to give up and die is like cheating.

PROVISIONS FOR THE AFTERLIFE

It was sensible of them,
to send goods with the dead.
Once we would pack baloney sandwiches
and plaid thermoses of sweet tea
for a trip that meant missing lunch.
Toilet paper, too. And pillows.
A first aid kit.
One never knew.

Now even on my bad days
I can walk to Dollar General,
and the grocery sells everything
but peace and gold. There's even—
three blocks away—a coffee shop
with walnut-cranberry scones.

I can barely thread a path
through home, I'm so prepared.
When I'm done, burn my body
to vapor and ash.

THE STARS ARE ALL DEAD AND HAVE FALLEN

And with help we loaded the pickup
with all the other things that no longer functioned.

Washing machine that shook itself to death.
Ancient computer, face like dirty city ice.
One stained mattress, upon which no children
were conceived. And so forth. Drove

somewhere. Nothing there but hills
someone had burned with cigarettes.

Thorns survived. And kudzu. There was a ditch
where an old Chevrolet dammed the runoff
and buried itself in red mud. There we did
our unloading. Appliances rolled downhill

like snake eyes. Newspaper bundles and slick
magazines fell like bad cards. Sliding down,
the mattress ripped some kudzu cover away
to expose layers of garbage. Households like ours.

A daughter's bicycle with glossy mylar streamers
looked to have been almost new, but vines
threaded its spokes and frame,
stitched it to the earth like Frida Kahlo.

We have returned our portion.

ABOUT THE LANGUAGE. AND INEVITABLE DEATH

Once upon a time
                    (and this is before you or I
or your mother or the dry disappearing women
who live under bridges were born)
                              words—some
words—had meanings unlike today's.
                              Night, for instance.

And Alone. Alone, alone could fill all the space
between all the yellow cities on the map with a hollow
more empty than the echo of the emptiest of moved-from homes,
dust where the dresser was, a penny, half a toothpick.

But we live in pre-owned valleys and cook
on the stove that came with the house.
Wearing heirloom language to work, to regret,
to shop for our suppers, we name common things.

And say we die and go to heaven.
Call the yellow night sky black.

Acknowledgments

Jim, Misky, Kory, Rita, Glenn: here it is!

Thanks are due, and to more people than can be named. But I'm going to try.

One day near the dawn of time, someone left an Ogden Nash book on top of the *Farm and Gardens* and *Field and Streams* on the settee at the farm. Whoever you were, I hope Heaven is all you expected.

In 1972, somehow convinced that poets wrote because they had something important to say, I gave up writing, having no earthshaking insights. Thank you, NaNoWriMo, for the fun and love and unimportance of being an amateur.

Internet prompt sites like *Writer's Digest's Poetic Asides* blog—thanks, Robert, for the PAD challenges—and the still-mourned readwritepoem helped me find my voice and gave me wonderful friends.

The Southern Festival of Books and the Scarritt Bennett Center introduced me to flesh-and-blood poets. Thank you, Joyce Sohl.

TJ Jarrett, Christina Stoddard, and Jeff Hardin put together a weekend generative workshop at Scarritt Bennett one October. That was like the best sort of candy sampler: some of every good flavor, plenty of nuts, and none of the stale gummies. That was a taste. David Baker and the Kenyon Review Writers Workshop turned out to be a meal, a life experience.

Jeff was also one of my MTSU Writers mentors and a terrific teacher. Kory Wells was my other mentor. The manuscript she helped me to put together is the backbone of this book. Thank you again, Kory.

Gianna Russo and her Yellow Jacket Press chose my chapbook manuscript *Testify* for their Peter Meinke Prize in 2018, even though almost none of the poems had seen publication. Gianna led to Madville. Double thank-you.

And: Brenda, Mary, Audrey, G'anne, Manuel, Sugar, Leslie, Jessie, Amy, David, Misky, Margo, and Barb.

Publication Credits

Some of these poems have appeared in other forms and with other titles, and I gratefully acknowledge the editors of the publications here.

"24," *qarrtsiluni*

"About the Language. And Inevitable Death," *Poetic Asides*

"Barefoot Madrigal," *Poem*

"Blues for the Fisherman," *Kairos Literary Magazine*

"Chas. Bukowski Works" and "I Never Dreamed I'd Be This Old,"
    Light: A Journal of Photography & Poetry

"Cynthia" and "[In fact I was not there]," *Curio Poetry*

"Drink/Word," *Right Hand Pointing*

"Fig," *Poetry Quarterly*

"The Island" and "The Stars are All Dead and Have Fallen," *Gnarled Oak*

"Lamentation," *Gutter Eloquence*

"A Miser's Life," "Ontology," and "Sustenance," *Red Wolf Journal*

"What's Put Away," *Bohemia*

"When She Was Venus," *CSHS Quarterly*

The chapbooks *Like a Movie. Like a Mary Sue* (Dancing Girl Press & Studio, 2018) and *Testify* (Yellow Jacket Press, 2018) contain many of the poems above.

About the Author

Barbara E. Young was born in a Nashville, Tennessee, that was nothing like today's city. She wrote poetry in high school, won a contest with a disappointing prize, went away to a small Baptist college. The nineteen-seventies are a blank during which she gave up writing in the belief that poetry should have something important to say, and she had nothing. Years later she discovered writing prompts, decided that important things were overrated, and eventually—having found no other calling—began to admit to being a poet. She, husband Jim, and their two cats live in White Bluff, near Nashville.

www.ingramcontent.com/pod-product-compliance
Lightning Source LLC
Chambersburg PA
CBHW031147090426
42738CB00008B/1253